GIFTED CHILDREN

THE CLEVELAND STORY

THIS PUBLICATION IS MADE POSSIBLE BY THE
CLEVELAND WOMEN'S CITY CLUB FOUNDATION

Sharing experiences

Gifted Children

THE CLEVELAND STORY

BY THEODORE HALL

THE WORLD PUBLISHING COMPANY

CLEVELAND AND NEW YORK

Library of Congress Catalog Card Number: 56-5308

THIRD PRINTING

The lines from *The Prophet* by Kahlil Gibran are reprinted with the kind permission of the publisher Alfred A. Knopf, Inc. Copyright 1923 by Kahlil Gibran; renewal copyright 1951 by Administrators, C. T. A. of Kahlil Gibran Estate, and Mary G. Gibran.

3HC1057

*It is when you give of yourself
    that you truly give;
There are those who give with joy,
    and that joy is their reward.*

KAHLIL GIBRAN

Contents

FOREWORD

By Charles H. Lake

Superintendent of the Cleveland Schools (1933-1947)

THIS BOOK is the story of the way the Cleveland Public Schools Major Work program discovers and educates the gifted child. The Major Work program was initiated by Mrs. Benjamin Patterson Bole some thirty years ago and has gone forward with ever-increasing success to the present time. The history of Mrs. Bole's work in this project is a heartening story of self-effacing devotion to, and consistent effort for, an ideal. It should give us all courage for renewed efforts in the field of education.

In our democracy it is sometimes difficult to avoid confusing the ideal of "equality of opportunity" with the general principle of "equality" as applied to social conditions.

Our children are not born equal in natural abilities, and the longer the educative process is continued the greater these inequalities become. True education develops inequalities: the inequalities of individuality, the inequalities of work and production, the glorious inequalities of talent and genius that we find in many fields of creative endeavor. The true measure of progress in our country must lie in such variations in abilities as opposed to mediocrity—in the advantageous use of individual abilities as contrasted with stultifying standardization.

Mrs. Bole, with a rare appreciation of the needs of our country, social, economic, and spiritual, realized the seriousness of this educational problem and resolved to try to do some-

9

thing constructive to help solve it. She strongly believed that some way should be found to discover, and then to develop and utilize, the abilities of our most able young people if we were to attain our potential stature as a nation. This belief was quite in contrast to the educational theories of some educators of a half-century ago, who maintained that the brilliant pupils would get along very well anyway and that teachers might well spend their time on the less able ones. Mrs. Bole believed that the potential services of many of our ablest young people were lost to us because of the lack of opportunity afforded them to develop their special talents. She was convinced that the only young people in our educational program who were being denied our vaunted "equality of opportunity" were the most able ones. Her thesis was this: an extended and thorough education for all the "able" and not alone for those who were able to pay for such an education.

The Women's City Club of Cleveland was prominent in the early development of Mrs. Bole's project. She discussed her plan with the members of the Board with the result that a Committee on the Supernormal Child was appointed, with Mrs. Bole as its chairman.

The project was approved and accepted by the Cleveland Board of Education in the summer of 1922, and has been a successful feature in the program of education of the Cleveland Public Schools since that time.

Mrs. Bole was one of those rare individuals whose discontent with things as she found them led her to work assiduously and constructively to make them better. She sought no credit for herself, but from the time the Major Work program was started she gave much time, thought, and material assistance to it.

This book is in her memory and honor.

GIFTED CHILDREN

THE CLEVELAND STORY

CHAPTER I

A Morning with Gifted Children

❦

At nine thirty on a morning last May, in one of the Major Work classrooms in George Washington School on the west side of Cleveland, a nine-year-old boy named Dan pushed back his chair from a work-table, stood up, and calmly announced: "Now it is time for the Morning Talk."

For half an hour the room had been quiet, but not absolutely quiet in the drillmaster sense. Four or five children, one after the other, had come up to Miss Kennedy* at

* A fictitious name.

her desk, had shown her papers or an open book, and had asked her questions on their work-in-hand in normal, un-awed voices. There were no duplicates among their questions for the simple reason that there were no dupli-cates in what they were working on.

Most of the children—the room held thirty-one, di-vided among second-, third-, and fourth-graders—re-mained grouped around their worktables in visibly steady application to a book, or a pencil, or a crayon, or a paint-brush. Once in a while a child would put some question about his work to a tablemate. This did not even draw a glance from Miss Kennedy. A boy walked over to a win-dow and asked the nearest group if they would mind if he opened the window wider. A very small girl, feeding some guppies in an aquarium, squealed and giggled when she dropped the spoon into the tank and had to reach under water for it. Two adjacent tables of children laughed with her, and Miss Kennedy looked up and smiled. She hadn't spoken a word to anyone beyond her desk since the first "good-morning's" of the day. She hadn't even told the children to sit down to their work.

Dan, in the fourth grade, was the class president. When he stood up to announce the Morning Talk he had taken his cue from a Program for the Day written on the black-board. Miss Kennedy had written this the previous week, but she had not decided it. The program was a joint decision of teacher and all the children in conference, and next week, if a majority wanted the program changed, it would change.

At Dan's words there was a general movement. A table—there were no old-style school desks in the room—was swung around parallel to a side wall, and two chairs were placed behind it. All the other chairs in the room were turned to face this table, and promptly occupied. To one of the chairs behind the table came a slight girl bearing an armload of books and of pictures mounted on cardboard. She had a red ribbon in her black hair, and a numb, rather glazed look on her face, and when she sat down she gazed off into space.

Dan stood by the other chair. "Will the class please come to order. [This was sheer formality.] Have you ever wondered where we got our American flag? And what its different parts mean? And what our flag was like when our country began, and all that? Well, Sally has chosen that subject for her Morning Talk today. We all know how hard Sally has been working on her facts, and I am sure she is going to give us a very interesting talk. Her title is 'The American Flag and Its . . .' "

Pause. " 'Ee-vo-lish-un . . .' "

Grin. " 'Ev-o-lish-un . . .' "

Another grin, with chortles from the older children. "I mean 'Ev-o-*loosh*-un!' . . . You know, I learned that new word yesterday, but I guess I didn't learn it good enough."

"*Well* enough," said Miss Kennedy. More smiles, with Dan joining in.

There is something that needs mention about these children. As you know, in measuring a child's intellectual power by the Stanford-Binet test, an IQ or intelligence quotient of 100 means average intelligence for the child's age. Raise the figure to IQ 125—an intelligence equal to the average of children 25 per cent older than the given child—and only one in fifty children has such a mental endowment. An IQ of 150, far rarer, is said to mean "genius." Now the fact is, every single child in this room before us, as in all other Major Work classrooms in Cleveland, has an IQ of 125 or higher. In Dan's audience there are three children with IQs of over 150. Dan himself has the incredible and almost frightening IQ of 163. At nine years of age, he possesses the mental powers of the average fifteen-year-old.

But is he a "child prodigy"? Is he one of those lonely, grim, dried-up, utterly tragic little figures, out-of-step and separated forever from their mates of human flesh and blood? On the contrary. You have just been watching as balanced and happy and normally adjusted a grow-

ing youngster as you would want to find anywhere—
and that fact, repeated with but few exceptions through-
out some sixteen hundred of these gifted children, is
enough to be the great glory of the Major Work program
of the Cleveland Public Schools.

We have left little Sally to stand up and twist her
fingers a moment and then plunge bravely into her talk.

It was a very good talk, I thought, but we are going
to let the children themselves do the judging, as is the
practice. Sally was soon over her shyness. In her hands
she kept an outline typed on file cards, and every few
sentences she looked down for guidance. Her talk lasted
ten minutes, and when it was done she held up the
mounted pictures one by one to show the successive de-
signs of the flag. Then she said, "Here are my references,"
and displayed four or five books with a brief description
of each. Then she sat down and folded her hands on the
table.

Dan stood up. "Thank you, Sally. I think that was an
interesting talk. I learned a lot of new facts. . . . Now,
everybody, how are we going to evaluate her talk?"

He turned to the wall behind him where, under a large
label "Our Morning Talks," a couple of posters were
mounted. One was a hand-drawn calendar of the month,
marked on each school day with the name of the child
and his subject for the scheduled daily talk. Another

was a hand-lettered list of nine questions. (These will be given in full in a later chapter; here we shall touch upon only two or three.) Dan read the first question aloud: " 'Do we have poise?' "

A boy at the back said, "I think Sally had good poise. Better than I had yesterday." Smiles around.

A girl: "I think she was a little nervous."

Another girl: "Right at the beginning, maybe. Then she got all over it. I think that means excellent poise."

Dan said, "Is that all? . . . Then let's vote on it. How many think Sally gets a 'three' for excellent poise?" Almost all the hands went up. "Or a 'two' for good poise?" A sprinkle of hands. "Or a 'one' for fair poise?" No hands. Dan leaned forward and penciled a "3" on a mimeographed form on the table.

Not until the hands went up for the voting did I think of the fact that these school children had been speaking up without raising their hands, and keeping turns by their own doing. It had all seemed so easy and natural.

"Now," Dan read it from the poster, " 'do we have worthwhile facts?' " Much nodding of heads, small discussion, and another "3."

" 'Do we have visual aids?' "

"Yes, of course," said a girl. "I think that's a silly question, unless they don't have any at all."

Another said, "She had so many pictures. I say excellent."

A boy asked, "Dan, wouldn't it be important how she *used* the visual aids?"

Dan found this a new one. After a moment he nodded. "Very important, I guess. What do you mean, Ronald?"

"Well," said Ronald, "I agree that Sally gave an excellent talk and told about all those flags. Then at the end she showed us all the pictures. But wouldn't it be better to see each picture when she talked about that particular flag? I got kind of mixed up."

Emphatic nods all around. When the vote came, it was "1" for fair. Sally gave Ronald a brief look. Then she smiled and said, "I wish I'd thought of that myself."

After all ten questions were put, Dan added up the scores and turned to the teacher. "Sally gets twenty-six, Miss Kennedy. That's a B."

Miss Kennedy opened her record book and duly entered the B. In these Major Work classes the children themselves do almost as much grading as the teacher.

"Tomorrow," said Dan, "Peter is going to talk to us about a famous sailor and fighter for England, Sir Francis Drake." The Morning Talk period was over, and the chairs went back around the tables, and the children sat down to their work again.

Miss Kennedy asked if I would like to explore the room, and she called up two children. "These are James and Norma," she said, "our class host and hostess." So a little guided tour. Any visitor to one of these Major Work classrooms would be struck by the wealth and variety of materials, resources, and exhibits at hand. Here are the highlights:

In one corner of the room was the Library Corner, set apart by settees and bookcases around a reading table, and enlivened by flowers, potted plants, goldfish in a bowl, and fanciful comic figurines. Behind all this was a gay mural, done by the children in poster paint on butcher paper, of a Chinese street scene. Perhaps 150 books stood on the low shelves: fairy stories, biographies, histories, travel books, a good child's encyclopedia in many volumes. Decidedly unexpected, the big Webster Unabridged dictionary lay open on a stand, looking half as big as the small boy using it.

At the next table two small girls were pecking away at typewriters. Not a usual fourth-grade sight, either. Beside them other children were busy and undistracted at a table strewn with books and papers, with more books standing in the center.

Next came a large globe, with a very tiny girl fingering Africa.

Then the aquarium.

Along the next wall were large hand-lettered posters, like the Morning Talk poster, that explained in simple numbered sentences: "Our Reading Club"—"Our Rules" —"Our Leader"—"Preparation for Discussion"—"Evaluate Discussions"—"My Responsibility." Each poster was headed with a gay and genuinely childlike painting of a classroom scene, obviously done by different hands.

Next, a piano.

Then a terrarium holding newts and a box tortoise.

Then the blackboard with the Program for the Day, and the classroom officers: President, Vice-President, Secretary, Treasurer, Guild Librarian, Room Librarian, Program Director. Under this was written: "A good citizen is kind and considerate of others. He does right because it is the right thing to do."

Next a progress chart with stars opposite the children's names, headed: "We Know How to Spell."

Another progress chart: "Facts in Arithmetic."

Still another, by date and for the class as a whole: "Our Attendance Record."

Now, before a sign saying "Today is Bank Day," a group of children were counting money at the tables, checking and rechecking the count, making entries in savings-bank books, and marking up the totals by denomination of coin in columns and lines ruled on the blackboard.

Then, at two tables pushed together, children were painting large and varied posters, with handsome travel posters from Japan, Sweden, and Sicily mounted on the wall behind them.

And last a bulletin board labelled "Science Today," upon which still more children were pinning clippings from newspapers and magazines, clipped at home, that ranged from "Electric Coal-Digging Machine" to "New Uses for Wonder Drugs."

The array was a little bewildering. But the class host and hostess knew about everything and were proud as Punch to show everything. "And this isn't all," James said. "Tomorrow we're going out in the woods to study trees, and next week we're going to visit a nut-and-bolt factory."

"I," declared Norma, "like trees a whole lot better than nuts and bolts."

Behind me Miss Kennedy was starting another activity. "It's time for today's Reading Club," she announced. "Will the members please come down to this end of the room?"

About a dozen of the smaller children picked up their chairs and arranged them near her desk in a circle, and then went back for books and papers. Miss Kennedy explained that these were second- and third-graders. When they were all seated, she asked, "Now who is today's leader?" There was a chorus of "Louise!" and a plump little blonde girl blushed and grinned.

"And how do we begin, Louise?"

"Oh," Louise started off in a singsong rush, "I'm supposed to tell the name of the book, and who it was that wrote it, and who it was that did the pictures, and—" She stopped short and blushed again.

"That's right," said Miss Kennedy calmly, "it's always good to stop and think. But it's better to think before you start. You know exactly what to do, so why not do it?"

Louise sat back in her chair and took it easier. She gave title and author and illustrator, and then burst out: "And it's all about giants, and a prince and princess, and all that—but Miss Kennedy, I'm supposed to say *when* it all happened, and I don't know!"

"Does anybody know when this story happened?" Miss Kennedy asked.

The children looked blankly at each other. "Fifty years ago," came one voice. "A hundred years ago," came another.

"You're just guessing," said Miss Kennedy mildly. "You're not really thinking."

A long pause. Then a little redheaded girl spoke up: "I don't think it *ever* happened, really and truly—so how can we tell *when* it happened?"

A slight little boy with glasses hurried in his words. "Ellen is perfectly right. This is a fairy story. But it has very many interesting things happening in it, and I enjoyed it very much, and I think that is all that matters."

Everybody nodded.

"Aren't there some kinds of stories," asked Miss Kennedy, "where it matters very much when they happened?"

Several eager voices started at once, and then there was sudden silence, and fidgeting, and sideways glances.

"Excuse me, Ellen," said a chunky boy carefully, and Ellen said, "Yes, Carl."

"Well," said Carl, "it's awfully important in history stories to know the year."

Ellen said firmly, "Are you through, Carl?" Carl nodded, and Ellen went on, "We ought to know the right years in biographies, too. So we don't put the Wright brothers back in the time of Benjamin Franklin."

"Does everybody agree?" Miss Kennedy asked. After a murmur of assent, she took up a piece of paper. "Here is our first question for today: 'Prove that the giants were helpful, kind, and powerful.'"

What followed this and succeeding questions was not in the least a recitation from memory. Each child, along with his copy of the storybook, held a sheet of notebook paper folded like a booklet that bore, on its cover, the handwritten title "Reading Club," followed by the name of the book. Inside the booklet each child had ruled a number of columns, headed in turn: "Question"—"Page"—"Paragraph"—"Remarks." Each question or part of a question had a crossline of its own, on which the child had written an answer by an exact reference to the book by page and paragraph, with added comment if desired. A child's preparation was all in his little written index of answers.

At the first question a boy spoke up. "I think the giants were helpful because . . ." and he referred to his index ". . . on page nine, paragraph two, it says . . ." and he opened the storybook and read aloud the sentences that applied.

"That's certainly a good proof," said Miss Kennedy. "Who found another proof?"

Silence, and much looking around.

"Didn't all of you answer that part of the question?"

Unanimous nods, and a few small, embarrassed smiles.

"You mean," with mock horror, "you mean that every single one of you chose that very same paragraph for your answer?"

A burst of laughter, and much squirming in chairs.

Miss Kennedy smiled drily. "One thing we are working for, you know, is originality—but I suppose on this answer the less said about that, the better."

The children settled back.

There was plenty of originality in answering other questions. Reference after reference was given and read aloud, most of them accepted by the group, but some drawing argument.

"What qualities did the prince have?" was one question put to the group, and a large girl with bangs spoke up: "The prince was young. It says so on page six, paragraph—"

"But wait!" Ben, the slight boy with glasses, broke in. "I don't think 'young' is a quality!"

"It certainly is," the large girl said. "If it isn't a quality, what is it?"

"Well," said Ben, "a quality is—is what makes people different. It's how you tell people apart."

"That's right. The prince was young—so you could tell he wasn't old, couldn't you? Isn't that—?"

"No—no!" Ben cried her down. "*Everybody* who's young is young. That doesn't make them different people. I mean, a quality is things like 'brave,' or 'generous,' or 'polite.'"

The girl smiled quickly. "Oh, I see. You mean not everybody is polite."

The whole group broke into laughter, with Miss Kennedy joining in despite herself. Then she said, "Let's call that enough on the subject. You know, both of you may be right about 'quality'—that would be a good word to look up in the big dictionary. And also," she smiled, "perhaps *both* of you, and the rest of us as well, need a little reminding about true politeness."

The discussion of the fairy story went on, not in answer to special questions from the teacher, but on more general questions that were apparently applied to every storybook read. Which parts were best liked? Which were adventurous, or happy, or sad? Which were true to life? Which were not understood? And what new words were found? All of this, again, was answered by specific references from each child. The book-in-hand may have been a fairy story, but it was remarkable what children and teacher drew from it together in judging and weighing human values and relations and motives. Besides, the story was fun.

When it came time for these children to evaluate their own discussion, they did it much on the lines of evaluating the Morning Talk but without the grading. Were we all prepared? Did we all contribute? Were all our contributions worthwhile? Were there any interruptions? (Laughter again.) Was there sharing? Was the leader prepared? Some rather candid remarks were voiced (said a girl, "I think Ben argued more than he contributed") but the general tone was notably unstrained, balanced, tolerant, and thoughtful. One needed to pinch oneself to recall that these were children of seven and eight years.

Then the Reading Club session came to a close, and the children took up their chairs and returned to their individual pursuits.

The morning was about over. But it seemed a good idea, before it was ended, to look over the shoulders of some of these children and see exactly what they were working on by themselves.

The large girl with bangs and the slight boy with glasses had made a beeline for the big Webster, to clear up the meaning of the word "quality."

Carl was reading a child's history of the Civil War. He was going to report on it next week to the room.

Ellen was crayoning a large panel of gay and shining butterflies.

Louise and Peter were giving each other a spelling drill, taking turns in reading the words aloud from the spelling book.

James was working up a Morning Talk on dinosaurs, and poring over colored pictures in *Life* magazine. He said he liked dinosaurs very much but there were an awful lot of them.

Norma was struggling over a poem for the school newspaper. It was about trees.

Ronald was filling up a notebook with simple experiments in physics. A page was headed: "Contraction and Expansion of Gases," and the first experiment read: "Take hard-boiled egg and peel it. Heat milk bottle under hot-water faucet. Stand egg in bottleneck. When bottle cools, egg will be sucked in."

Dan was helping Sally with her multiplication table. She said nothing bothered her much except the nines. She couldn't keep the nine-times's straight. Was nine times nine 81 or 82?

"Look, I'll show you something," said Dan. "I just noticed it one day. Write the answers to the whole table down like this: 18, 27, 36, 45, 54, 63, 72, 81, 90. Maybe it won't help you, but it's pretty neat. Take the first answer, 18, and add the two digits together: 1 and 8 are 9. Take the next, 2 and 7 are 9. Take the—"

"Nine! Nine! Nine! . . . " Sally went on adding like a flash, and laughed with delight. "Does it keep on after the 90?"

"I don't know," Dan admitted.

"Why, it's *interesting!*" Sally cried. "Let's go on and see what else we can find about it!"

As a motto for these gifted children in the Major Work program, we might leave it at that.

CHAPTER 2

The Gifted Child by Himself

THE GIFTED CHILD is a child—only more so.

I do not mean childish; I mean something very different. The gifted child is more *childlike*. He has and retains more of the two main qualities that seem the essence of childhood, and that are too soon smudged over and weakened and all but lost in the average child.

The first of these qualities is the sense of wonder and curiosity. All normal children have this. It is as natural for a child to be eagerly and keenly interested in just about everything under the sun as it is for him to like lollipops. Why? . . . How? . . . Where? . . . and the rest of Kipling's "six honest serving-men"—these are at the core of the child's mind. And yet—how soon, in so many children, this hunger to know and to understand starts to fade away! We all know too many children who seem interested in less and less as they grow older, and who come to take almost everything blandly and blindly for granted. But the chief mark of the gifted child in the Major Work program is the continuing freshness and breadth of his interests.

The second main quality of childhood is creativeness, the desire and the power to make something new. Again this is at the child's core. Look at the young child with blocks, or crayons, or sand pile—almost all his play (that is, almost all his living aside from bodily necessities) is one or another kind of making, of free creation. Every normal child does this, and he brings this freedom of creation with him when he enters school.

Then something begins to happen. A few more years and the creativeness of most children, in nearly everything they are required to make or do, is about as free and original and true to themselves as if they had copied it, in every jot and tittle, out of a book of directions. But this freedom of creation very noticeably stays with the gifted child in a Major Work class. Not just in art or poetry or story-writing or such, which we too often think are the only creative subjects. To work out an outline for a Morning Talk on the history of the flag, or to compose a report on the latest labor-saving machinery for the farm, is just as creative as painting a picture. Creation, at bottom, is simply thinking for oneself.

I do not want to give you the impression that we are dealing with little geniuses, with little paragons of intellectual perfection and perfect behavior. These Major Work children are just as various as any children. They can be as childish as any children; they can have their sulks or tantrums and commit their selfish or thoughtless or cruel little acts, the same as any other child. They have their weaknesses, and make their mistakes. They are children—not specimens. If we keep all this in mind, we can go on and feel a truer appreciation of the qualities and skills these children develop in a Major Work classroom.

Take initiative. We all know that not many traditional classes give evidence that such a quality exists, but Major Work gives it special attention. For example, the twenty-minute talk given once a semester by each child is of course an assignment. But after that it is all up to him. He sets his own date for the talk. He chooses his own subject, out of his own interests, and goes into it in his own way. He searches out his sources and materials for himself. He can ask his teacher for advice, but he is never told exactly what he should do. He works all that out for himself—which is the only way there is to develop initiative.

Then there is the ability of these gifted children to manage their own time. We have seen that the school day has its program, a program set up by the children and the teacher in conference. But within that program the children soon learn to budget their time and apply themselves to study with considerable maturity. And they do not flare up and then fade down on a large project; they carry it along with commendable steadiness from week to week. This capacity stems partly from the long attention-span that is a mark of high IQ children, but even more from the keenness of interest that they can bring to many sides of a subject. Their absorption as they bend over their worktables is an impressive sight. No one could push a child into that; it is their interests pulling them.

The gifted child, these Major Work teachers will tell you, is distinguished from average children in still other ways. He has an unusual ability to generalize, to take a number of facts, even seemingly unrelated facts, and find a common meaning in them. He can see the parts, but he can also see the picture as a whole. He is able to judge something pretty well for himself, remaining skeptical until good proof is given. He can make comparative evaluations, often in complex matters. When called upon, he is able to offer another child criticism and suggestions that are genuinely constructive, largely because he can so easily imagine himself in the other child's shoes. We glimpsed some of these intellectual abilities in the first chapter.

But intellect is not everything. The way art is taught these Major Work children does not differ materially from the regular curriculum, but it seems both more personal and more wide-reaching. The teachers aim at making school art a part of living for every child, not just an activity for the specially talented. Technique and finish and accuracy can all come later; the starting point here is the basic value of art—its power to release tensions and express emotions. All children need this. Yet perhaps the gifted child, because he is exceptionally intelligent and sensitive, needs it the more.

For children in the earlier grades, the teacher will begin an art class by reading a story or poem or by playing some music on the phonograph, to create in the children a mood that can help release emotions. Then the children draw their impressions, always encouraged by the teacher to create from their own experience and environment. At other times the teacher will ask them to draw something that makes them angry, or happy, or afraid, or sad, or that illustrates such feelings as mystery or loneliness. When a child is troubled, just putting such a drawing down on paper can give him enough emotional release to be of great help in itself. The drawing can also offer a revealing insight into the child, aiding the teacher to understand him better as an individual.

Art not only helps bring the child to a better adjustment inside himself, it goes on and enriches almost all his school projects. Creative drawings and paintings are constantly being made in close connection with everything from social studies to literature and even science. Some of this art work may be much "better" than others, but each creation is the child's own, important in his rounded development, and so every sign of originality is warmly encouraged. The child is also taught that art is not just something beautiful on paper; it can be all around him in the arrangement of a bulletin board or of the whole schoolroom, it can even be in his own posture or tone of voice. Art, the gifted child comes to learn, is harmony, inside and out.

Making things with his hands seems particularly satisfying to the gifted child, no doubt because of his interest in creating new things and expressing new ideas. These children do excellent work in the handicrafts, using simple tools in wood, metal, plastic, and textiles. There are no class projects; each child chooses his own, with the one important proviso that every article he makes must be useful. Craft work helps these gifted children to relax emotionally but still be mentally alert. It also teaches them that it takes careful planning, hard work, accuracy, and patience to produce satisfying results.

Music is taught in a five-point program: singing, dancing, listening, playing, and creating. Gifted children seem outstanding in folk dancing and other rhythmic activities. Music appreciation begins in the fourth grade, with special concerts for all Cleveland school children given by the Cleveland Symphony Orchestra. In preparation, the children listen to recordings of the scheduled programs and learn to recognize the instruments and their musical effects. Music teachers say the response of these gifted children to classical music is enthusiastic and unusually perceptive. In Major Work, music enters into a number of other subjects, such as social studies where folk music and folk dances help in the understanding of various nationality groups. Even elementary schools have their bands and orchestras; 41 per cent of the Major Work children in a recent year were studying an instrument in school time. These gifted children are perfectionists at their instruments and easily discouraged, but once they feel confidence they progress rapidly. On the creative aspect of music, many young children like to make up their own tunes, and Major Work helps them all it can in this. Not many keep it up. In this day the child is so constantly surrounded, not to say bombarded, by the set musical compositions of others that he soon feels no need for making his own tunes. Probably no other creativeness disappears so fast and so completely.

There is another side to "the gifted child by himself": his feelings about himself as a gifted child. He certainly knows he is gifted—he would hardly be gifted if he didn't!—and here he is in a selected class, in a program of study with the imposing name of "Major Work," that is shared by only 2 per cent of Cleveland's school children. Many people ask, "Doesn't this make him conceited? Doesn't this give him a superiority complex?"

The Major Work teachers have a simple answer. They point out that the one surest way to make this gifted child conceited is to leave him in a class of average children, where chances are he will have no least rival, where he will finish his work far ahead of everyone else, where he will be the one child in the room who knows all the answers and who can speak up on almost any subject. *That*, they say, is the way to breed conceit.

After all, superiority is only relative. When the gifted child sits in a Major Work classroom, he finds himself among children who are equally or even more gifted. Even if he has the highest IQ in the room, the others have quite enough to give him plenty of challenge and keep him working.

It must also be pointed out that these gifted children are not isolated all day in their Major Work classroom. They take a full share in the general activities of the school. They play in the playground and go to physical education classes in the gymnasium with all the other children in the building. They join in the choral groups and the school orchestra or band; they are members of the safety patrol and of student council; they work on the school paper and compete in the school spelling and poster contests. Only in their schoolwork do they stay in a room of their own.

One other question is asked by many people: "How well do these gifted children know their drill subjects?"

The answer of the Major Work teachers is much like what the mother in *Our Town* said of her daughter's prettiness: "Enough for all normal purposes." These children know their drill subjects well, but not startlingly well. They learn what they need to know for carrying out their various projects or units of study. They meet the standards for their grade, which are the same standards as for average children. Their purely scholastic achievement, in fact, does not begin to approach their high mental ages—which is just the way the

Major Work Department wants it. An eight-year-old with an IQ of 150, and who matched that with the scholastic achievement of a twelve-year-old, would most likely not be a rounded, well-adjusted child but an unhappy prodigy.

So the great emphasis in Major Work is on the qualities or attributes of the truly educated mind: interestedness, creativeness, initiative, the powers of correlation and evaluation and independent judgment. The mind needs its working tools, yes. But to store facts is something else.

May I put a small test to you, a doubtless very well-educated reader?

Did you once study chemistry?—Please now describe a common method of making sulfuric acid. . . .

Did you study Latin?—Please decline *aestus*. . . .

Did you study American history?—Please list the main points of the Treaty of Ghent. . . .

Education, as someone well said, is what remains when the facts are forgotten.

CHAPTER 3

The Gifted Child with His Classmates

THE BOOKS TELL US that man is a social animal, but you would never know it in the old traditional classroom. A child spoke only when he was directly addressed by the teacher, or when he first raised his hand and was then given permission to speak by the teacher. If one child spoke a sentence to another child, that was a felony, and if the second child replied in even the rudiment of a conversation, that was a high crime like treason or piracy. Perhaps I exaggerate. It all seemed normal enough when I was raising my own hand over an ink-stained desk, and it probably still seems normal to several million school children around the country. But it does not seem normal, or anything like normal, after you have visited a Major Work classroom. Then only the natural, easy, considerate, purposeful, and self-responsible social relationship of these gifted children, among themselves and with their teacher, seems normal.

"We talk a lot," one Major Work child told me.

They certainly do! But it is not set and formal recitation—there is little if any of that in these classes—and it is not idle chatter. These gifted children practice and enjoy a kind of talk that is a miniature of the "good conversation" so many adults yearn for, and so seldom find.

This practice in talking together comes in a variety of ways. A group of children may talk about some hobby or special interest they have in common. Regular sessions take place in social studies, current events, science, and history, and all these give plenty of grounds for lively discussion. The regular Reading Club is another conversational forum, and so are classroom committee meetings of all kinds. There is a great deal more stretching and exercising of young minds in all this than may appear.

Some very sound principles run through these discussions and conversations. Of course it is the teacher who first implants them, not by dominance but by quiet suggestion. "If you want to have a good talk together," she will say, "wouldn't it be better for each of you to be prepared with something to contribute? . . . If you want to enjoy your talk, wouldn't it be better not to interrupt each other?" One rule always observed is that each discussion group shall have a leader, whose task is not to shine by his own light but to bring out the best in the others.

This is a remarkably adult responsibility for any boy or girl. The leader sees to it that the discussion keeps on the track, bringing it back when some remark might confuse the issue or change the topic too soon. He sees to it that every child has a fair share in the talk, learning to draw out the reticent by a simple "What do you think, John?" He reminds the over-voluble that there are others who have something to say. When interest seems to lag, the leader may put in a sharp question, or set the group laughing with a light remark. The key to the leader's competence in all this is the fact that the leadership rotates. Every boy and girl in the group will have a turn, they all come to learn the ways and means of sharing a good discussion, and so when they are not the leader they are quick to respond to him for the good of the discussion as a whole.

You must not think that even a gifted child can learn these skills and attitudes overnight. Yet it is surprising how early they can be learned reasonably well. The Major Work child starts this training in the second grade.

Few visitors fail to be impressed with the way these gifted children can stand up before the class and give a clear, well-spoken, and interesting talk. Even the youngest children show little of the self-consciousness so common among much older children, in traditional classes, who get no instruction in the art until junior high school. The daily Morning Talk—whether the twenty-minute talk once a semester, or the more frequent five-minute talk—is one of the most valuable features of Major Work.

Every child in every class gives a talk in due turn. The teacher carefully explains the steps toward such a talk, and an outline is posted on the wall:

PREPARATION FOR TALK

1. Choose a subject.
2. Limit your subject.
3. Gather information: books, people, places.
4. Put information in order.
5. Present talk.

The child bases his talk on research or actual experience, citing authorities when necessary, and showing illustrative materials of every sort. A boy may talk about home experiments in electricity, and demonstrate a solenoid coil or lamps wired in series and in parallel. A girl

might tell the story of volcanoes, with blackboard drawings. Book illustrations are commonly shown for any
subject; it was a special occasion when one girl brought
Mexican costumes and pottery, gathered on family trips,
to illustrate a talk on Mexico. Then there was the sixth-
grade boy who had marked the wall calendar for his
coming talk with the one word "Chiroptera." That may
not have sent these gifted children to the big Webster,
but it sent me. It means "bats," and his illustrative materials were alive.

After the child selects and organizes his information,
he typewrites an outline on 3 x 5-inch cards, including
dates, figures, and direct quotes to be used. Often, as a
starter, he will type out his opening sentence. But no talk
is ever memorized; the child speaks from his outline,
making up his sentences as he goes along, for firsthand
effectiveness.

In all this the child takes on full self-responsibility.
No one prods or reminds him. On the day that the child
has selected, the teacher and class expect his talk. Afterward, as we have seen, the class discusses and criticizes
his talk, and then it votes on the grade the child will
receive.

To guide each child's efforts, a check list of aims is
agreed upon by the class and the teacher, and posted on
the wall. This list is typical:

Do We Have:

1. Poise?
2. Worthwhile facts?
3. Visual aids?
4. Distinct speech?
5. Good English?
6. Careful preparation?
7. Correct length?
8. Interesting topic?
9. Notes in outline?

The items on the delivery of a talk bring out a special point. To a child, his distinctness and modulation and freedom from mannerisms and even his correctness of grammar and pronunciation are so personal that only a few teachers (and even fewer parents) can comment on his failings and errors without stirring up some degree of resentment. Apparently a child feels little or no resentment over such comments from another child; they are accepted as constructive criticism from an equal. Sometimes these gifted children are able to teach each other as nobody else can.

All Major Work children learn to talk well before a group, but the most skillful among them have the chance to speak before a group that includes thousands of other Cleveland school children.

Radio station WBOE, owned and operated by the Cleveland Board of Education, broadcasts regular educational programs to all grades in all schools, with children taking a large and active part. Many children are used in dramatic skits, which are written to include many young parts. Children also take part in panel discussions and act as program announcers. When WBOE auditions the skilled children who are referred to it, and lists the satisfactory children to call on when needed, it is not looking for stars; it is trying to spread the benefits of radio work as widely as is feasible.

The Major Work children take this radio work in stride. Since the programs are usually recorded before broadcasting, the young performer can sit with his classmates and listen to himself speaking over the air. Then come the candid comments: "I think Johnny spoke too fast. . . . I think he dropped his voice too much at the end of his sentences. . . ."   "I think so too," sighs Johnny. "But just wait until *you* talk into a mike!"

In one special kind of talk the Major Work program was a pioneer in the country. Only lately have other public elementary schools begun to teach a foreign language. For many years now, the Major Work children have all studied French.

But "study" is not the word—these children absorb

French the way a sponge absorbs water. The way they are taught takes advantage of the psychological fact, not often utilized, that up to the mental age of eleven or twelve a child can learn a foreign language directly, naturally, without self-consciousness, almost without effort. He accepts the foreign words and foreign sounds without question. His ear is keen and so is his gift of mimicry. He likes to repeat what he hears, and go on repeating it, without a thought in the world that he is practicing and memorizing. This is exactly the way that he learned to speak his own language when he was very young.

So the Major Work program makes full use of these receptive, so-called bilingual years. The teachers of French are special teachers, not home-room teachers, who take each Major Work class in all grades for forty-five minutes each day. They teach no grammar, no reading, no writing. They teach French simply by speaking French, which takes very skillful teaching indeed. The teacher uses gestures, actions, pantomime, sketches on the blackboard—anything to avoid English words—in order to convey her meaning while she repeats the particular French word. No doubt some English is inevitable at the very beginning, but it is surprising how soon the teacher and these gifted children are speaking nothing but French to each other. The children learn *within* the language, just as they learned English.

Before long the children have built up a vocabulary based on familiar experience: home, toys, clothing, school, games, animals. Out of this comes the telling, in French, of such well-known stories as "The Three Bears" and "Red Riding Hood." Simple gesture games are played in French, and French songs are sung. Later come dialogues, and little plays in which each child learns every part. In all this the teacher is encouraging a constant but flexible repetition, so that the children, always hungry for new material, will still have the feeling of novelty while they are really only practicing the same stage of learning in a different way.

The goal of these French teachers is to help each child, within the vocabulary of his daily life, to speak French fluently and correctly, and to understand it with spontaneous recognition. How well these gifted children succeed in this is apparent to any visitor. And also how greatly they enjoy it.

Now we come to writing.

If you ask a professional writer if he thinks writing is fun, he will look at you with pity and amazement. Fun! ... Way over on the other hand, these Major Work children take a lively and sustained joy in writing. Out of a number of reasons for this contrast, just one concerns us here: the distance from the audience. The professional adult, while writing, is so far from his audience that he never knows for sure that he has one. His daily work has all the socialness, all the warm sharing, of the daily work of the oyster.

Now watch these Major Work children. They sit side-by-side at their tables, scribbling away together. They smile suddenly at a happy idea, get it down on paper, and nudge a neighbor: "Wait until you read *this*!" They write in the midst of their audience; each child is writer *and* audience. And they can hardly wait to finish their pages and, either by reading aloud or by posting their scripts on a bulletin board, start sharing in a give-and-take of warm, immediate, and very human reactions. In short, their writing is fun because it is an immediate social communication, a live social activity.

These gifted children are highly creative, but they still need encouragement to write creatively. Their teachers well know that the creation, the desire, the inside picture of what the child wants to convey in his writing, gets bogged down and lost if there is too much emphasis on the rules and techniques of writing. The teachers certainly recognize that the child needs to learn these basic matters. Neatness and legibility, spelling, sentence and paragraph structure, punctuation, grammar, clarity and coherence and all the rest—all these are taught the Major Work children. But, and this is a tremendous "but," they are taught as means and not ends. They are taught as necessary means by which the child who enjoys his writing can communicate that enjoyment far better—and thus write far more effectively—to any audience. And the child learns these matters not in chunks, but as he needs and uses them.

So the Major Work teachers insist that writing should never be done just for the sake of practice, or to teach rules and techniques. Each child should come to his writing filled with his own creative purpose. Let him pour out his thoughts on paper; the polishing comes afterward. Without this first full flow there is nothing worth polishing. Which is why the Major Work teacher is careful to accept the child's piece of writing as a whole, welcoming the big creative things to praise before she picks out the little things to criticize and correct.

Early in their schooling these children use their writing skill in several directly social ways. The desire to write letters comes up naturally, and does not have to be assigned. But the teacher must lead the child to a respect for the various forms and styles required by different kinds of letters, from an informal note to a friend all the way to a request for information from a public figure.

One Major Work class sent this last kind of letter to Dr. Ralph J. Bunche, whom they were studying, and then sent him a thank-you letter when the information arrived. Later they sent him a congratulatory letter upon his Nobel Peace Prize, and were in seventh heaven to receive his thanks on U.N. stationery.

Hardly any other form of writing can be so social, or provide such fun, as the writing of little plays and skits. These gifted children delight in doing this, and they do it well, even in the earliest grades. To sit down in a group and make up the lines together, then to divide up the parts and plan the action, and then to act it all out with their own chosen words in front of an audience—could boys and girls want more? Without spoiling the children's enjoyment, the Major Work teacher can tell you that writing, producing, and acting in a play makes a unified approach to the entire area of the language arts. Plays have good use in the large group-work unit, as we shall see in the next chapter.

One special form of writing is perhaps the most important of all in the education of children. Poetry came long before prose in the history of the human race, and poetry is just as fundamental to the child. Poetry teaches the magic in words—the very essence of speaking and writing—as nothing else can. It is a very rare (and unfortunate) child who does not take to making verses as naturally as he breathes, and who does not enjoy poetry as naturally as he enjoys play or sunlight.

The Major Work children come early to poetry, finding in it a kind of living-together as a group while they listen to the teacher read it aloud. Soon they are choosing their favorites from the wide range of children's poetry, probably first for story or mood. But with familiarity they move on with awareness and appreciation to the matters most distinctive of poetry: rhythm, rhyme, the music of alliteration and assonance, personification, simile and metaphor, the striking imagery of the one true word. The technical terms are not exhilarating; the poetry itself is. Children realize quite early that poems are delightful because poets use imagination in the *way* they say things.

Very soon these gifted children want to use their own imaginations. As a simple first step the teacher may name a quality such as "softness of sound," and even the youngest children will respond with some simple image: "a kitten's purr," "a gentle rain." She names more qualities, and gets more responses. And then, on the simple pattern of Hilda Conkling's "I Am," the class together will couple their phrases for their first little poem:

> *I am the morning dew*
> *For freshness.*

I am a bubbling spring
For coolness.
I am a gloomy night
For blackness.
I am new-fallen snow
For whiteness.

And with that most children are off on their own. They build on other simple patterns suggested by the teacher. They come to rhyme and meter and all the rest when they are ready. They find out about the structure of poems, and how the last lines pull the whole together. They discover that their best poems are made out of their own feelings and thoughts and discoveries, and that this intensely personal quality is what makes a poem alive and interesting.

Many poems by Major Work children would be worth quoting here. Let me give you just one and tell you why a literary critic would call it remarkable. It comes out of a common daily experience, fused with a newly-discovered (for the author) scientific fact—and adult poets seem to touch on science at their peril! The tone of childishness occurs only at the beginning, then turns to childlikeness. It depends not at all upon the sometimes cloying similes and metaphors of the young. It is done in the most difficult of poetic styles, the poetry of simplicity and plain speech. And it ends—many an adult poet would envy this—with a consummate handling of monosyllables.

The poem is by a fourth-grade girl. It seems that her Major Work class visited the Cleveland Museum of Natural History and were much impressed by a lesson on stars and their distance in light-years.

LITTLE STAR

Little star, shine oh, so bright,
Little star, shine through the night!

Each shining beam of light, I know,
Started earthward long ago.

But when your silver rays I see,
It seems they're shining just for me.

It is as though you know I care
When I look up and see you there.

CHAPTER 4

The Gifted Child and the Outer World

The world is so full of a number of things," sang Stevenson—but it is not we adults who are made as happy as kings by this, it is these gifted children in Major Work. Their wonder and curiosity about a very great number of things is extraordinary. A high IQ may not cause a high degree of curiosity and interestedness; in fact it might well be the other way around, with the extra curiosity producing the high IQ. But we'll leave that to the psychologists. It is enough to note here something of the gifted child's range and variety of interests in the outer world.

This was made particularly clear during a visit I paid to one Major Work classroom of fifth- and sixth-graders. These children, aged ten and eleven, had been constructing models and other visual demonstrations in the field of science. One by one they stood up to explain their handiwork, and if they were proud, they had a right to be.

Rose-Marie had made an elaborate map of the country showing where the various types of soil occur. She used scientific terms for these soils that I had never heard of.

Arthur had made a mobile, very gay and colorful, on the sources of light: sun, stars, flame, electric filament, radium paint, a firefly. Maybe there were more.

Eugene had made a cut-away model of the human heart, about the size of a football. It was quite as impressive as something you see in a health museum. Materials included plaster of Paris, window screening, plastic tubing for veins, a carved turnip for something else, and candles warmed and then bent for arteries. Only he said things like "vena cava" and "aorta."

Helen demonstrated the subject of vision and color by various devices. She showed us the mixing of pigments; the mixing of light by spinning discs; the eye's fatigue, on staring at one color, that will produce an afterimage of the complementary color—and other matters even more abstruse.

David had made a model of the solar system. It was not exactly to scale, but then you could hardly get a true scale model onto a football field.

Harvey had built, for eight dollars he'd earned by his paper route, a one-tube radio set that worked nicely. He had become interested by watching a radio "ham" who lived next door, he had studied up on the subject, and he told us that a radio wiring diagram in a scouting manual, of the set he'd chosen to build, had mistakes in it. Then he drew the right diagram on the blackboard, with explanations. I did not try to follow. Along with 998 other adults out of a thousand, I could not draw even the most elementary diagram to show how radio works.

And as a last sample of what can interest a gifted child, Genevieve had taken a cardboard packing box and made a diorama of the strange, luminous fishes at the bottom of the ocean. It was beautiful, and it cost fifty cents for the paint.

As handiwork, these various exhibits must have been great fun for the children to make. But there is rather more to the picture. Each project, if you will glance back over the list, must have depended upon each boy and girl having an unusual skill and ease in traveling through the world of books. You will not find soil geography or abyssal fishes or the theory of color vision in the first book at hand.

It is in the field of reading, as any Major Work teacher will tell you, that these children far outstrip other children of the same age. Many a fifth- or sixth-grader in Major Work reads something like two hundred books a year, or four a week the year around!

They start in very young. Many of these gifted children are able to read when they enter school, so they do not need that concentration upon reading skill that marks the traditional classroom. Of course they are all taught to read increasingly well. But the goal with these children, from the beginning, is to develop their personal and permanent interest in the whole wide world of books.

Now the last thing a Major Work teacher wants is to develop a bookish child: a child who reads a book, and then another book, and another, just reading the books and nothing more. The Major Work child is saved from this rather narcotic path by the same means that helped make writing fun. Reading is made a social experience; the process of reading is not complete until the child actively shares the fruits of his reading with his classmates. Those science models and exhibits were nothing if not an active, vivid, even tangible sharing of each child's reading.

But the chief device for this sharing is the daily Reading Club. We saw one in action in the first chapter for second- and third-graders. Even children so young, as you noticed, did not talk about the story itself, on the level of merely telling each other what happened. They all knew what happened. Instead, they were bringing forward their own personal opinions and judgments and feelings about the story, in lively and thoroughly healthy comparison. At other times the children even go into such matters as the author's way of introducing new characters, or his efforts at building suspense. Many an author would be amazed to hear very young children carefully analyzing his writing techniques. Every elementary classroom in the Major Work program, from second through sixth grade, has three or four Reading Clubs to keep the groups small and informal. Discussion in the higher grades becomes very keen and competent indeed. From youngest to oldest the children take this motto: "It is what I think and how I feel about what I read that is important."

Another form of sharing a book is the written book report or review, with the same emphasis upon independent thinking and feeling. Still another form is the scheduled Poetry Meeting. Perhaps the day's opening period once a week will be given to a program of poetry read aloud, with five or six children taking part, and often the teacher. This is one of the best-liked features of the week.

The cry that children today do not care for the classics of literature, the Major Work teachers will tell you, does not apply to these gifted children. The teachers find that these children readily appreciate and enjoy the beauties of great literature. Another field of special interest is biography, in which the children not only discuss the life and achievements of the subject but also the skill and particular slant of the biographer. These gifted children seem to have an unusually keen admiration for the great figures, past and present, and their private emulation is no doubt considerable.

For all this reading there is a wealth of books in every Major Work classroom. These include the books regularly supplied to all classrooms by the Board of Education, and still more books, of greater variety and challenge, provided by the Major Work Department. On top of this, the Cleveland Public Library gladly loans up to 150 books a month to a class. And sometimes, for special projects, all this may not be enough, and so every Major Work child is taught and encouraged to use a public library by himself.

One of the goals of Major Work is to start developing good citizens in the democratic way of life, and here the teaching of current events comes to the front. Once a week the children in each class, in all grades, join in a discussion on several current topics. These may have been chosen from a weekly news digest to which everyone subscribes, or from the weekly broadcast, "Behind the Headlines," which is aimed at fifth- and sixth-graders by Cleveland's school radio station, WBOE. A News Chairman and a small News Committee, rotated each week so that all the children may have the experience, select the topics. Each member of the committee is responsible for one topic and starts to gather clippings, pictures, and other reference material on it. The others in the class are invited to add material for any topic that interests them. Then the committee selects the best of all this to mount on a bulletin board as background for the lively discussion in the current-events period. Afterward the material is filed for future reference.

Other methods of teaching current events may be chosen by pupils and teacher. In fact current topics may come in as background to almost any project or work-unit. Whatever the method, the aim is to bring out in each child an ability to read the news critically, with an independent mind, and an awareness of the way the events of city, state, nation, and the world link together. This is the way to start making a responsible citizen.

Children may not get very far out into the world. But

all this flow of books and other materials can bring much of the world to them.

Now it needs repeating that many if not most of the things done in a Major Work classroom are also done in a traditional classroom. The difference here is the *way* they are done. The enrichment of the curriculum that you find here means not only the range of activities from French to typewriting, from science exhibits to the writing and staging of plays. Enrichment very particularly means the breadth of interest, and depth of attention and understanding, that these gifted children can bring to a single theme. We have seen something of this in the Morning Talk, especially the twenty-minute talk that can take weeks to prepare.

But an even better example is the large unit of group work, which can call out the interests and efforts of every child in a Major Work classroom for two or three months on end. Only gifted children could accomplish this, let alone enjoy it.

As one Major Work teacher put it, "Learning should be experience. That's the only way anyone can keep hold of the knowledge, skills, and attitudes he acquires. And that experience should be varied. What the child needs is a wide area of knowledge and experience and activity that grows spontaneously out of a single theme.

The teacher guides—but it is the child's personal interest, his personal participation, that carries him through to the end."

Let us come down to cases and take a good look at one group-work unit, to see what these gifted children can get out of—or rather, put into—a single theme.

This particular Major Work classroom held thirty-five children, about evenly divided among fourth-, fifth-, and sixth-graders. One March, as the seventeenth drew near, the children noticed the green decorations in the store windows and the Irish music on the radio. Some child suggested they have a Saint Patrick's Day party, and so they did. It was very simple: a couple of Irish songs, the reading of an Irish folk tale by the teacher, and some green-decorated cookies from home. This much would be quite usual in any traditional classroom. Now all resemblance ceases.

Next day, during a chat with his teacher, a sixth-grade boy remarked that his mother had forbidden him to play with another boy because the boy was Irish. He said he didn't know any Irish personally, but he'd heard they were "a wild and uncivilized people."

The teacher laid this statement before the children in a class-wide discussion. "Do we have anyone here of Irish blood?" she asked them. A Riley and a Connolly promptly spoke up—much to the surprise of the sixth-grade boy, who had never thought of these classmates as Irish. German and English names made up most of the rest, with one Slavic, one Czech, and two Hungarian. "Let's all make a family tree of ourselves," said the teacher. "Ask your parents when you get home."

The result astonished everybody. No less than 40 per cent of the children had at least one Irish ancestor.

Then the 6A Reading Club decided to read "Cuchulain," the saga of an ancient Irish hero. They enjoyed this so much that it started the fourth- and fifth-graders reading Irish fairy and folk tales. A group of the children then visited the Irish Cultural Garden—one of Cleveland's unique series of nationality gardens that celebrate old-country leaders and events—and came back with an interesting report. The 6A group thought that parts of "Cuchulain" should be dramatized, maybe for graduation. The younger children wanted to join the fun. . . . And suddenly, in the midst of a class-wide meeting, an entire project was born: the children decided with enthusiasm that their June graduation exercises for the whole room would be an All-Irish Program.

You noticed how small and casual was the beginning of this project, and how it started with the children and was gently taken up by the teacher and then continued by the children. What followed was an immense, complex, all-embracing, and highly enriched unit of group-work—though no child ever thought of it that way. But as the project grew and grew, and as the teacher guided it, she had *her* objectives. They were:

A. To develop the spirit of understanding other people.

B. To call out every skill in the class, and to give the children as wide a variety of experiences as possible, as they studied Ireland and its geography, resources, people, history, art, music, literature, and so on.

C. To have each child realize the contributions of the Irish in America, and thus appreciate our country as a land of liberty and opportunity.

When the All-Irish Graduation Program was ready in June, it was presented twice: first for representative Clevelanders of Irish descent along with Major Work administrators and visiting teachers, and the next day for the children's parents and friends. It began with a three-word address of welcome in Gaelic (*Cead mile failte!*—"A hundred thousand welcomes!") and ended with the singing of "God Bless America." It was made up of twenty-eight items, of which no less than sixteen were talks. There were talks on everything from "Ireland Beautiful" to the "Gaelic Language," from "Pagan Ireland" to the "Irish in America," from "Ireland's Problems" to the "Gaelic Revival." There were pageants, dramatizations, songs, dances, displays of pictures and maps, and recitations and readings. Every child in the room took part.

But that wasn't all. Around the classroom, at the time, were paintings, posters, sand-table models, and physical and political maps, all on the theme of Ireland. There were telefact charts of the 1820–1940 immigration figures not only of the Irish but of every nationality represented in the room. There were the letters of the Gaelic alphabet cut large from green paper and mounted, and pictures of Irish scenes clipped from steamship and travel-agency booklets. And in the place of honor was a display of Irish articles that had been handed down in the children's families from their Irish ancestors. The display ranged from linens and Belleek dinnerware to an array of school copybooks made by the grandfather of one of the children when he was a boy back in Ireland. Grandfather himself was there too, and mighty proud.

What had the children done to prepare for all this? Just about everything! After it was all over, the Major Work Department made an outline of this group-work unit that runs to twenty-two single-spaced pages. So I must leave something to the imagination of the reader, and bring up just one aspect.

"But where are the school subjects?" some parents are sure to ask.

They were right there, studied every day, but almost invisible. The children were so interested in the *substance* or *content* of what they were doing that they quite forgot they were studying school subjects. Every skill they used was a school-subject skill: reading (their book list held forty titles), speaking, writing, letter writing (invitations, and requests for material), geography study, history study, research techniques, library use, literary and art appreciation, music, drawing and painting, handicraft (costumes and scenery), and so on. Even arithmetic: the children could not find the cost of materials, or measure this or that, or prepare statistics for an immigration chart, or work out the percentage of Irish in any area, without using—which means studying—arithmetic.

All this is what a group-work unit means.

And the unit held values not always found in a school subject. Take that sixth-grade boy who started the ball rolling, and his mother too—I doubt that they ever again thought of the Irish as "wild and uncivilized."

CHAPTER 5

The Gifted Child and the Major Work Program

❧

When little mary came to first grade in a Cleveland elementary school, she could already read. Not just "Tom, see the cow." She could read simple fairy stories and work her way through newspaper headlines. As a word-sampling to show you here, Mary could sail through a printed riddle like "Question: What is the difference between a teacher and an engineer? Answer: One trains the mind, and the other minds the train."

Mary would laugh aloud over that; such plays on words delighted her.

She couldn't write, but she could make capital letters. She would letter out extremely simple little stories, inventing as she went, and draw the pictures to illustrate. Her spelling left something to be desired, but if she spelled it N-O when she meant K-N-O-W, some people would at least call that sensible. She could add 22 and 7, or 150 and 25, and take away 20 from 40, or 5 from 11.

No one had sat right down and taught her any of this. She had asked questions—the sands of the sea have about the same number!—and she had remembered, and everything she did was a kind of play. Pretty obviously she was a gifted child.

As a gifted child, Mary would have been left among the average in many a school system. But Cleveland was ready for her. In first grade, while her classmates were stumbling over "See how the cow runs," her teacher allowed Mary to read books that matched her ability. Yet even with some other special attentions, which could not be many in a large class, Mary did little but idle along ahead of the others. This was not in the least good for her, but a change was on its way.

One day the teacher gave every child in Mary's class a group intelligence test. In fact, every child in Cleveland in certain designated grades takes one of these tests. They are sent out by the school system's Bureau of Educational Research, with the aim of finding what is called the Probable Learning Rate for each child. The teacher lists these PLRs and sends them back to the bureau.

Now the winnowing starts. It is the responsibility of the Supervisor of Major Work to keep an eye on every child who has a high PLR. The principal of the school is also alerted, and so is the psychologist who is assigned to that school. When the child has a high PLR and is not overage for his grade, further testing is in order. Now the school psychologist administers the Stanford-Binet test for innate intelligence.

When a child is average in intelligence, his intelligence quotient or IQ rating on this test is from 90 to 110. When his IQ lies between 110 and 120 or so, he is considered a good bright child or what the school system calls a "high X." These high X's, though ahead of the average, are not held back by the regular curriculum. They are often gathered in "Enrichment Classes" which use the regular curriculum along with a few of the features of Major Work.

But the child with an IQ of 125 or over is in a different situation. The regular course and methods of study, set up for the average, cannot offer the gifted child enough interest and challenge to bring out his abilities, let alone develop them. Why should little Mary idle along through the rest of her school years? She had a high PLR and an IQ of 148, and a Major Work class was indicated.

Was indicated—not automatically attained. We can now see more of the personal and searching attention that the Cleveland schools give to the gifted child. (They give just as careful attention to the retarded or handicapped child, but that is another story.) When the reports came in on Mary, her teacher and her principal and her school psychologist sat down together to talk about her. In many such conferences they are joined by the Supervisor of Major Work. As to Mary, they discussed everything they knew about her: her IQ as an indication of ability, her physical make-up, her emotional stability, her social adjustment, her home background, her special problems. They were not looking for perfection. They were trying to see Mary in the round as a whole child, and to understand, with a great deal of faith and hope, what the Major Work program might be able to do for her. They decided that Mary seemed to warrant the advantages offered by Major Work.

Did they then pluck Mary out of her regular class and plump her down with the special group? Not at all. The Supervisor of Major Work herself went to call on Mary's mother and explained the whole matter. The school principals share this task, but it is an index of Cleveland's methods that a large number of these calls are made by the Supervisor in person. Only when Mary's mother had understood the program and visited a Major Work classroom and consulted her husband and given permission, only then was it arranged for Mary to enter Major Work in the second grade.

A small point but an interesting one in these calls is that the mother always wants to know her child's exact IQ, but the caller never tells her. The child himself never learns his IQ. All they are told about it is "125 or over."

A big point is the fact that in most cases a Major Work child must change schools. There are not enough gifted children in a school to set up a Major Work class in each one. So these classes are centered in specially accessible schools, with the children transferring from surrounding schools. The parents must take the responsibility of getting the children to and from school. The children, unlike other elementary school children, may bring their lunches.

Another point explained to the mother is that no child in the Cleveland schools is "accelerated"—that is, moved or jumped a grade within any school year. A ten-year-old with an IQ of 140 has the intelligence of a fourteen-year-old. But physically and emotionally and socially he is still ten, and to put him in the older group would be to leave him a fish out of water. He needs to swim with his more general equals.

This grouping together of the gifted may also seem a kind of segregation. But the Major Work children, as we have seen, take a full part in all the school-wide activities. And this seeming separation is no more than that in any regular class taught by a single teacher. Actually, in Major Work, there is a kind of vertical fluidity, of give-and-take among different ages, that has disappeared from schools since the days of the "little red schoolhouse" with all grades in one room. Second-, third-, and fourth-grade children are commonly placed together, and so are fifth- and sixth-graders, with marked benefits for the younger at least.

All the Major Work described so far in these pages has been in the elementary grades, but the classes continue into junior and senior high school. Here, however, the distinctive features tend to fade out. It is still a grouping together of the gifted in a home room, but the necessity of teaching set subjects, by various teachers and in various combinations, makes many of the earlier methods impracticable.

There were twenty students in the first Major Work class back in 1922. Now in elementary schools there are 38 classes with about 1,100 students; in junior high schools, 18 sections with about 250 students; in senior high schools, 12 sections with about 250 students.

Every child in the program has his complete record

through the school years kept in a specially-designed folder. On top of this the Major Work Department maintains a very active follow-up. Each of the gifted students is given an interview just before graduation from twelfth grade, is assured of the department's continuing interest in him, and is asked to co-operate in the follow-up. Thereafter, twice a year by means of a return postcard, the department asks each graduate where he is at the present time, what he is doing, and how he is getting along.

The department stresses the continuing flexibility and improvement of the Major Work program. Nothing in it is fixed. Spanish may be taught some day instead of French; one subject may be introduced earlier, and another one later; one method may be dropped, and another one begun. No administrator or teacher in Major Work believes for a minute that they have the last answer to the education of the gifted child. They are still searching, and they will keep on searching.

The teacher herself is the key to the whole Major Work program. She must have traits and abilities desirable in all teachers, but especially needed for teaching gifted children. Mastery in one or more fields is a requisite, but she is not there in the classroom to show that off. She is there to be concerned with each child as a distinct individual, to draw him out with sympathy and understanding, to help him develop better personality habits and better work habits, to encourage his ideas and his creative efforts, and to recognize his good work. Or to put it all in three words, she is there to *appreciate each child*. That is the only known way to get the best from a human being. But how many people can do it? The wonder is that the Major Work Department has been able to find and train so many teachers who do it so well.

As for these gifted children, you can well imagine how they come to regard these teachers. One small boy, as his mother reported, had put the picture of his Major Work teacher up on his wall, right beside "Hopalong" Cassidy.

A Guide

FOR DEVELOPING CLASSES FOR GIFTED CHILDREN

A Guide

FOR DEVELOPING CLASSES FOR GIFTED CHILDREN

DOROTHY E. NORRIS
Supervisor, Major Work Classes

I. *Philosophy of Major Work Classes*

    A. Conserving our greatest human resources
    B. Providing opportunities for the development of abilities of individual pupil
    C. Training for leadership in a democracy
    D. Developing individual potentialities for service to society

II. *Initiating Program for Major Work Classes*

    A. From interests within school system
    B. From gradual realization of need
    C. From demands of
        1. Parents
        2. Teachers
        3. Community
        4. Civic groups

III. *Observing Characteristics of Potential Candidates for Major Work Classes*

    A. Physical development—energetic
    B. General intelligence
    C. Power of analysis—asks "why?"
    D. Power to reason
        1. Interprets ideas
        2. Sees likenesses, differences
        3. Generalizes
    E. Originality
    F. Initiative—desire to challenge, to prove, to find out
    G. Ability to adjust
        1. Socially
        2. Emotionally
    H. Sustained attention-span
    I. Avid interest
    J. Keen observation
    K. Ability to evaluate personal activities

IV. *Selecting Candidates for Major Work Classes*

    A. City-wide group intelligence testing program
    B. Appraisal of maturity
        1. Social adjustment
        2. Emotional adjustment
        3. Sense of responsibility
    C. Teacher's judgment
        1. School achievement
        2. School adjustment
    D. Age-grade status
    E. Physical fitness
    F. Parents' opinions—story of babyhood and childhood
    G. Maladjusted candidate
        1. Immature
        2. Social or emotional maladjustment
        3. Poor school achievement and adjustment
    H. Individual psychological testing
        (In Cleveland, the individual Binet test is administered

by a certified psychologist, IQ 125 required for entrance into a Major Work class.)

V. *Choosing Teachers for Major Work Classes*

A. Experience
1. Successful teaching of average students
2. Two years classroom teaching or more
B. Faith
1. In superior ability of some children
2. In training for leadership
3. In challenging potentiality
4. In fostering ideals of democracy
C. Training
1. In child development
2. In educational psychology
3. In psychology of individual differences
4. In counseling
5. In teaching methods
D. Characteristics
1. Personality of teacher
  a. Sense of humor
  b. Warmth of personality
  c. Professional modesty
  d. Self-confidence
  e. Sympathetic attitude
  f. Open-mindedness
  g. Experimental attitude
  h. Freedom from jealousy
  i. Joyous attitude toward life
  j. Ingeniousness, resourcefulness
  k. Fairness and firmness
2. Attitude toward teaching
  a. Interest in children
  b. Willingness to accept children's ideas
  c. Interest in acquiring breadth of information
  d. Recognition and acceptance of some children's superior intelligence
  e. Satisfaction in children's achievements

3. Physical attributes
    a. Good physical health
    b. Good mental health

VI. *Selecting Equipment for Major Work Classes*

A. Furniture
    1. Tables and chairs
    2. Discussion table (preferably round) and chairs
    3. Cupboards
        a. For children's supplies
        b. Low
        c. Kindergarten
        d. Partitioned
    4. Open bookshelves
        a. For reference sets—encyclopedia
        b. Single copy library
            (1) Fiction
            (2) Supplementary
    5. Easel
    6. Workbench
B. Equipment
    1. Typewriter
    2. Microscope and supplies for scientific experiments
    3. Maps
    4. Globes
    5. Charts
    6. Tools for woodworking

VII. *Setting Up Teaching Groups for Major Work Classes*

A. Where?
    1. In buildings where principals and staff co-operate (on common philosophy)
    2. In buildings having a nucleus of high IQ pupils
    3. In area accessible to public transportation
B. How?
    1. By canvassing neighboring school buildings for high IQ students

2. By combining high IQ students from grades 1, 2, 3
3. By combining high IQ students from grades 4, 5, 6
4. By organizing high IQ students in first and highest section in junior and senior high school
5. By keeping class size to 25 pupils
6. By combining grades and divisions in elementary buildings
   a. To facilitate teacher preparation
   b. To save time
7. By discussion with parent about—
   a. Fast-thinking child (not too different from average)
   b. Enrichment of program
      (1) Foreign language
      (2) Special art, music work
   c. Stimulating school climate
   d. Training for leadership
   e. Similar ability of classmates
   f. Voluntary acceptance of program
   g. Responsibility of parent toward the program
      (1) Modest attitude
      (2) Presenting new program to child

C. By whom?
   1. Supervisor, full- or part-time
   2. Committee of entire staff

VIII. *Orienting the Major Work Class*

A. As integral part of school
   1. By participation in all school activities
   2. By participation in instruction by school specialists
B. By maintaining school routine
C. By being subject to same school records
   1. Report cards
   2. Attendance records, et al.

IX. *Enriching the Curriculum for Major Work Groups*

(Cleveland's definition of enrichment is attempting to develop methods of teaching which are aimed at meeting the individual needs of these students.)

A. By broadening the regular course of study
B. By enriching
    1. Through art
    2. Through music
    3. Through foreign language
       (In Cleveland, French is the foreign language taught. A special course of study in the conversational aspect of the language has been written for these classes. Specially trained teachers of French conduct this phase of the program.)
    4. Through field trips
    5. Through community association
C. By classroom methods
    1. Through discussion
       a. Of problems
       b. By pooling ideas
       c. By drawing conclusions
    2. Through the "know how"
       a. Of finding information
       b. Of giving talks
       c. Of doing research
       d. Of evaluating
       e. Of experimenting
       f. Of listening
       g. Of observing
       h. Of interviewing
       i. Of writing
       j. Of outlining
D. By use of charts
    1. Individual
    2. Class
E. By using units of work based on interests of children

X. *Initiating Follow-up for Major Work Class Students*
    A. Record secured from returned addressed postcards
       1. Questions on card

    a. Name
    b. Address
    c. Where employed?
    d. Position?
    e. Where in school?
    f. Present status
    g. Training for what?
    h. Present ambition?
    i. Remarks: (Marital status, family, important events, etc.)

B. Postal cards released biannually

C. Study of data in progress

ACKNOWLEDGMENTS

GRATITUDE is extended to Dr. Mark C. Schinnerer, Superintendent of the Cleveland Public Schools, whose staunch support has been invaluable in carrying out the Major Work program for Cleveland's gifted children.

Special acknowledgment is made to Dorothy E. Norris, Supervisor of Major Work Classes, who pioneered with Roberta Holden Bole in the belief that the challenge of gifted children should and could be met in public education, and whose warm understanding of gifted children, and devotion to them, has been at the heart of the Major Work program for the past thirty years.

The success of the program has rested upon the special skill and enthusiasm of the teachers of the Major Work classes, who have also helped to make this book possible by sharing their ideas and experiences.

Ruth Abraham
Ruth Bejcek
Dorothy Bliesch
Louise Brown
Carol Froehlich

Rose Gates
Lucy Goldrich
Olive Hackney
Therese Jacques
Helen Levstick

Gertrude Luther,
   Research Department
Grace Mills
Ruth Nelson
Isabel O'Neill
Helen O'Rourke
Cornelia Patrick
Beatrice Ritz
Florence Roach
Ruth Roediger
Rebecca Rosenberg

Josephine Rozko Rupp
Ophelia Smith
Catherine Staten
Helen Stolte
Florence Toaz
Alma Wanstall
Dorothy Watson
Helen Wicoff
Winifred Wiest
Mary Zachman

Due recognition is made to Dr. Emile B. de Sauzé, former Director of Foreign Languages of the Cleveland Public Schools, for his part in introducing the study of French in the elementary grades of the Major Work program.

CLEVELAND WOMEN'S CITY CLUB FOUNDATION

Theodore Hall was born in Ashtabula, Ohio, and attended the public grade schools there. He went on to Punahou Academy, Honolulu; Western High School, Washington, D. C., and Harvard College where he received an A.B. in 1930.

As a writer since then, he has been editorial assistant to Bernard DeVoto, research assistant to the late Mark Sullivan, daily book columnist on the *Washington Post* for three years, free-lancer, and staff writer in the Office of Civilian Defense during the war. He wrote a brief official history of Cleveland for its Sesquicentennial in 1946. He wrote the story of the Brush Foundation, Cleveland, and its twelve-year study of the well-developed child. With the late W. T. Holliday, president of Standard Oil of Ohio, he wrote a plea for world federation under the title "Our Number One Job: World Peace" that in booklet form, *Reader's Digest* condensation in world-wide editions, and coast-to-coast newspaper advertisements reached a total circulation of some 19,000,000 copies—the most widely read plea on the subject ever written.

At present he is the staff writer for the Cleveland City Planning Commission. He lives in Willoughby, Ohio, with his wife and sons of thirteen and eleven years and daughter of seven.